How To Support A Loved One With Depression

The Ultimate Guide on How To Help a Loved One With Depression

Edward Katherine

Table of Contents

Chapter 1

Understanding Depression

Depression is a frequent illness that we hear about yet have difficulty identifying, especially in ourselves. As a result, far too many people suffering from depression fail to seek appropriate treatment. However, by arming ourselves with information on the illness, we can learn to distinguish it from a simple case of the "blues," comprehend the symptoms and underlying causes, and so seek appropriate therapy. Remember that depression is prevalent, it is more than just feeling bad, and, most importantly, it can be treated.

Depression is a common yet deadly disorder that affects 21 million Americans every year. If you or someone you know is depressed, know that you are not alone. Nearly one out of every five people will experience depression at least once in their lives. Depression takes many forms, including anxiety, stress, insomnia, fatigue, vague aches and pains, and so on. It is one of the most common problems encountered by physicians.

Women experience depression at roughly double the rate of males. Hormonal fluctuations, low self-esteem, and genetics could all be contributing factors. Many women are especially vulnerable following the birth of a child. For some women, postpartum depression can be exacerbated by physical and hormonal changes, as well as the added stress of a new baby. While temporary "blues" are common in new mothers, a full-fledged depressive episode is not normal and requires active intervention.

Males are less likely than women to suffer from depression, although the disorder affects 6 million males in the United States. In reality, the suicide rate among men is roughly four times that of women. Men may be harder to diagnose with depression because they tend to show frustration, wrath, and discouragement instead of feeling powerless and hopeless. Furthermore, men are less likely to acknowledge depression, and physicians are less likely to detect it.

Even if a male recognizes that he is depressed, he may be less likely than a woman to seek help. Encouragement and support from concerned family members might have an impact.

Depression is a mood condition characterized by persistent feelings of sadness or hopelessness. It is critical to recognize the distinction between clinical depression and feeling the blues. Depression is more than just feeling down or having bad days; it is an illness that affects the body, mood, and thoughts. It influences how a person eats and sleeps, how they feel about themselves, and how they think about things. A depressive disorder is not the same as a temporary unpleasant mood, nor is it a sign of personal weakness. Many people with depression produce higher-than-normal levels of cortisol, a stress hormone that suppresses the immune system. People in poor health may seek medical assistance from a doctor if the underlying cause is depression.

There is also an association between stress and depression. There is a complex link between stressful experiences, our minds and bodies' reactions to stress, and the emergence of clinical depression. Some people may develop depression as a result of a stressful event in their lives, such as the death of a loved one, the loss of a job, or the breakdown of a relationship. Stress can also emerge as a result of a more positive event, such as getting married, relocating to a new place, or beginning new employment. Depression can be both seasonal and situational, with some people finding the bleakness of winter months especially difficult; this is known as SAD (Seasonal Affective Disorder).

The following are some key indications and symptoms associated with various forms of depression:

It's important to watch out for individuals you care about and understand the indications of depression in a loved one. If you are concerned that a friend or family member is depressed, look for the following indicators.

Consistently low mood

Depression generates a persistent and sometimes unavoidable bad mood. This is one of the most typical indications of depression in your loved ones. It is more than just melancholy; their low moods are marked by emotions of hopelessness, helplessness, and emptiness. These feelings are all-consuming, and there often appears to be no end in sight when deep in a depressive episode.

Fatigue or lack of energy

People suffering from depression frequently report feeling tired, drained, or lacking energy. No matter how much sleep they get, their exhaustion usually persists. It might occasionally show weariness, which makes it difficult to find the drive to do anything. This may prevent your loved one from wanting to get out of bed or leave the house for days at a time.

Excessive sense of worthlessness or guilt

Depression is defined by intense but irrational feelings of guilt, self-loathing, or worthlessness. Their condition indicates that they are lethargic, unmotivated, and not worth the time. It may attempt to persuade them that no one cares about them and that their loved ones are lying to them. This is one of the most distressing indications of depression to spot in a loved one. Convincing them that these things are not true can be tough.

Loss of interest or delight in activities they previously enjoyed

People suffering from depression lose interest or delight in many hobbies and activities they formerly enjoyed. Their bad mood and lack of energy make it difficult to find excitement in activities they used to like. These hobbies include exercising, playing an instrument, and socializing with friends. If your loved one withdraws from activities in which they previously participated, this could indicate that they are suffering from depression.

Difficulties focusing and concentrating

Depression makes it difficult to focus on even the simplest chores. It's difficult to concentrate for long periods of time when overpowered by a sensation of hopelessness or helplessness. These challenges have an impact on almost every aspect of a person's life, including education, career, and home life. They can cause problems in school or at work, causing people to lag behind on projects or tasks.

Feelings of frustration, irritation, and rage
Frustration, impatience, and wrath are prominent symptoms of depression for some people. Depression is a difficult condition to treat and cope with. Many people become weary while dealing with their symptoms, resulting in a short temper and sudden fury. Some people may feel misunderstood or that they are unable to discuss what is going on, exacerbating their aggravation.

Aches, pains, cramps, headaches, or stomach issues with no apparent reason
Although depression is a psychological condition, it can result in a variety of psychosomatic symptoms. A loved one showing signs of depression may endure a variety of aches and pains. They can experience headaches, cramping, or stomach issues. If these physical symptoms have no clear origin or explanation, they could be due to a mental condition.

Appetite or weight change
Depression-related psychosomatic digestive difficulties frequently cause hunger fluctuations. Your loved one may feel more or less hungry than usual. Some people limit their food intake, while others consume more than they normally would. These shifts in hunger lead to weight fluctuations. Sudden weight loss or growth is another indicator of depression to watch for.

Problems sleeping
Depression causes a variety of sleep issues. Some people sleep excessively, while others have sleep disturbances throughout the night, and some cannot sleep at all. People with depression frequently suffer all three types of sleeping problems at different periods. Irregular sleep patterns are among the most typical symptoms of depression. Poor sleep exacerbates other symptoms, and continuous weariness has a wide-ranging impact on the individual's life.

Thoughts of suicide

Suicidal thoughts are most commonly related to depression. It is one of the most dangerous symptoms of depression to watch for. It's difficult to know how serious your loved one is about carrying out plans. Suicidal ideation covers both suicidal thoughts and attempts.

Types of Depression

Major depressive disorder and persistent depressive disorder are two of the most frequent types of depression that people suffer, although there are numerous more types of depression. Major depressive episodes are common in the majority of mood disorders. This is also true for bipolar disorder, a different type of mood disease.

Major Depression Disorder

People with major depressive disorder have experienced at least one major depressive episode, which includes five or more symptoms over a two-week period. For other patients, this illness is recurring, which means they may have episodes once a month, once a year, or multiple times throughout their life. People who suffer recurrent episodes of significant depression are frequently referred to as having unipolar depression or what was previously known as "clinical depression" since they only experience periods of low or depressed mood.

Persistent Depression Disorder

Low-level depression that lasts for a long time and is chronic is called persistent depressive disorder, formerly known as dysthymia. Persistent depressive disorder causes a depressed mood that is less severe than major depression but can be just as problematic.

Postpartum Depression

Postpartum depression is defined as emotions of melancholy, indifference, tiredness, and anxiety that a woman may experience following the delivery of her child. It affects one out of every nine women who have given birth, and it can afflict any woman, regardless of age, color, or socioeconomic status.

Bipolar Depression

People with bipolar illness have mood swings that include both lows (bipolar depression) and highs (mania if severe, hypomania if mild). Bipolar disorder lows have symptoms that are remarkably similar to those of unipolar depression.

Seasonal affective disorder

Seasonal Affective Disorder (SAD) often begins in the late fall and early winter and ends in the spring and summer. Summer depression can occur, but it is considerably less prevalent than winter SAD.

Psychotic Depression

Psychotic depression occurs when psychotic symptoms, such as hallucinations and delusions, are combined with a significant depressive episode, despite the fact that psychotic symptoms typically include depressing themes such as guilt, worthlessness, and death.

Causes and Triggers

People can detect and be aware of signs of depression in themselves and others by identifying depression triggers.

Bereavement

The experience of sadness and loss is one of the primary situational triggers of depression. However, diagnosis can be difficult because the symptoms may simply be seen as a typical reaction to loss.

Grief is a personal experience. The way grief is managed is determined by the individual's age, life experience, personality, state of mind, and the incident being grieved. Grief can cause physical and mental symptoms, such as:

- ❖ *Anxiety*
- ❖ *Anger*

- ❖ ***Increased blood pressure and heart rate***
- ❖ ***High-stress hormone levels***
- ❖ ***Sleep disorders.***
- ❖ ***The immune system changes.***
- ❖ ***Substance use***

Complicated sorrow, also known as prolonged grief disorder, occurs when grief becomes extended or strong. Rumination can exacerbate the complexity of grief.

It might be difficult to determine when the normal sadness of loss spills over into depression. People who are mourning should communicate their feelings with their doctor, especially if they are having difficulty coping.

Rejection

People have a natural desire for praise, affirmation, and acceptance from others. Rejection and social exclusion can be extremely distressing for people and have been linked to low self-esteem. Some persons are extremely sensitive to social rejection, with a high rejection sensitivity (RS). A person's RS level is determined by their genetics and life experiences.

People with a high RS are more sensitive to social cues, picking up on even the least hint of rejection. They react strongly to any hints noticed. Any apparent failure to be accepted produces worry. With perceived repeated failures, social disengagement and sadness develop.

Even persons without a high RS can work hard to earn the acceptance of others and feel defeated when they are rejected. Rejection is very frequently accompanied by anger and hostility. This is especially true when the rejection comes from a romantic interest.

Depression, on the other hand, promotes an increase in RS because people suffering from depression have reduced self-esteem and are thus more susceptible to rejection. Their negative depressive symptoms, such as low mood, lack of energy, social isolation, and loss of interest in activities, may increase their chances of being socially rejected. The significant stigma around depression and other mental health conditions may increase the risk of rejection.

An individual's RS is not always fixed at a specific level. Counseling can help manage depression and prevent relapses.

Stress

Psychological stress is a leading cause of depression due to its physical effects on the body and brain. Stress, in particular, produces hormonal alterations, which are present in approximately 70% of depressed persons. The hypothalamus, pituitary, and adrenal glands are unable to regulate mood and emotion as they normally do.

Stress produces the stress hormone cortisol, which causes physical changes in brain cells. Stress can also cause changes in the size of the hippocampus, a brain region that is known to be diminished in depressive persons.

Psychological stress also activates the immune system, resulting in the release of immune system molecules (cytokines) that are linked to depression. These immune molecules are active in brain tissue, particularly the hippocampus, which explains why they cause symptoms of mental illness.

Illness

Illnesses may account for up to 10-15% of all occurrences of depression. This association may occur because:

The illness itself may be terrible, and obtaining the diagnosis can be stressful. Examples include cancer, HIV infection, and Multiple Sclerosis.

The sickness may produce depressed symptoms, such as hypothyroidism, vitamin B12 insufficiency, and mononucleosis.

The condition may have an inherent link with depression, such as Parkinson's disease, erectile dysfunction, and heart attacks.

Some heart drugs, hormones, and certain antibiotics may produce depression as part of the treatment for the illness.

There is a mutual association between disease and depression. Many illnesses or their treatments can produce depression, and depression has been linked to slower recovery and a higher risk of mortality in many illnesses. In the case of a chronic or fatal condition, co-occurring depression can exacerbate the suffering caused by the sickness.

Physicians should inform their patients about any illnesses or medications that may induce depression, and they should keep an eye out for these side effects. Similarly, those who are sick should be aware of this prevalent and devastating side effect of the disease.

Lack of sleep
Sleep and depression have a reciprocal link. First and foremost, sleep disturbances are a major indication of depression. An individual's sleep levels have either increased or reduced. Insomnia affects approximately 75% of depressed persons, while approximately 40% sleep excessively (hypersomnia), with significant overlap. Sleep issues are among the most common reasons people seek treatment for depression.

Conversely, depression has been connected to sleep deprivation. Insomnia increases the likelihood of developing depression by fourfold. Scientific research in adult twins found that five hours of sleep or less increases the risk of depression. Because these were twins, the hereditary propensity to depression was not a consideration.

Another big research on teens found that sleeping six hours or less per night increased the incidence of depression by 25% to 38%. Developing depression can disrupt sleep, resulting in a vicious cycle. Adolescents appear to be particularly prone to sleep deprivation, which is frequently self-imposed.

Addressing sleep issues looks to be an effective method to prevent depression, treat depression, and avoid recurrence. Furthermore, considering the link between sleep disorders and suicide risk, treating sleep complaints in depressed people is very crucial.

Rumination
Rumination is an uncontrolled expression of grief. The person who ruminates focuses on their pain rather than embracing and dealing with it in a healthy way. Grief and pain become obsessions that interfere with daily living functions.

Ruminators get hooked on ideas like, "Why did this happen to me," and, "How bad is this? They become caught up in self-pity and magnify the bad. They may also become enraged with people who are dealing with their grief in healthier ways. It's hardly unexpected that rumination has been identified as a primary contributor to depression. It can cause sadness, exacerbate and extend pre-existing depression, and increase the risk of suicidal ideation. In contrast, depressed people's inadequate emotional regulation can lead to rumination.

Grief is a natural part of life, but many individuals are unprepared to deal with it, especially if it is their first encounter. Their expectations regarding grieving may be unrealistic.

Researchers discovered that hope, internal confidence, and motivation to succeed are effective antidotes for rumination. People with strong hope have more self-efficacy and are more focused on moving forward with their lives despite the loss they are grieving, rather than ruminating.

Money Problems
Financial troubles can trigger depression in a variety of ways. A study of 35,000 Americans indicated that poor household income increases the incidence of mental health issues, particularly depression. The study discovered that a decrease in income raises the likelihood of depression.

Additional studies discovered that financial troubles and financial stress are linked to depression, which appears to exacerbate financial challenges, resulting in a vicious cycle.

People facing financial issues, such as income cuts or financial loss, may consider taking steps to increase their ability to manage the stress that comes with these changes.

Life Transitions
Even favorable life transitions might negatively impact a person's mood. People are creatures of habit, so even pleasant life changes can put them out of their element and generate stress.

For example, a work advancement may require leaving a known and comfortable position for one that is unfamiliar and tough. The new work may require you to leave familiar people and surround yourself with strangers. It may also be more stressful, with a steep learning curve. The cumulative consequence is stress, which may lead to depression, despite the pleasant event of being promoted. If the life transition is bad, such as losing a job or being divorced, the stress and depression will be even more severe.

A subtype of depression known as adjustment disorder occurs when an individual gets depressive symptoms or even complete depression as a result of life circumstances. People should anticipate and prepare for the stressors associated with life changes. Those who are having problems coping might consider contacting their support system and even seeking counseling. They should also keep an eye out for any signs of depression that may arise as a result of these life changes.

Substance Use
Substance abuse and depression are intimately linked. Many of the mental and physical changes observed in both depression and addiction are comparable. They also share numerous risk factors, have similar symptoms, and can cause or trigger each other.

Recent research has demonstrated that drug and alcohol usage can create physical alterations in the connections between brain cells, resulting in the formation of new pathways that promote addiction.

Many people use narcotics to self-medicate their mental health issues. In many cases, people are unaware that they have a treatable mental health issue and have lived with their symptoms for so long that they believe it is normal.

Comorbidity is defined as the presence of substance use and depression or other mental health conditions together. When comorbidity occurs, both conditions must be treated simultaneously. It is tough to cure depression while someone is actively using drugs. Similarly, attempting to treat addiction in the presence of untreated depression significantly reduces the likelihood of success.

Managing Depression Triggers

Increasing understanding of depression triggers is crucial to treating them because it enables sufferers and their loved ones to identify them and respond appropriately.

Even if people are confronted with a trigger that they cannot immediately change, such as chronic sickness, financial difficulties, or a life transition, they can take steps to lessen the stress associated with the event.

People who suffer from depression require professional help due to the wide range of severity and causes. It is a serious sickness that can progress to chronicity, resulting in disability, a lower quality of life, physical illness, and death. Comorbidity is particularly hazardous and necessitates expert treatment.

Chapter 2

Communicating Effectively

Knowing what to say to someone dealing with depression can be difficult. Perhaps you're frightened you'll say something wrong. Perhaps you'll say something that makes their day even worse? Perhaps you feel it would be better to avoid the person till they feel better? However, many persons with depression feel alone, which exacerbates their depressive episodes. We've compiled a list of communication guidelines to assist you talk with a loved one or coworker who is experiencing depression.

Begin by being honest
When you're having trouble talking to someone, it's always best to be honest. If you don't know what to say, just tell them, but make sure your friend knows you're there for them. This will assist in breaking the ice, and you may find it easier to communicate freely going ahead.

If you truly understand or can sympathize, tell them so. While your intentions are noble, you should never claim to grasp a problem if you lack experience. Instead of saying "I understand," try expressing "I can't imagine how difficult this must feel." Your honesty will be greatly appreciated.

Tell them that you care about them
Words are really powerful. "I care" might mean everything to someone who feels alone or as if the world is against them. A hug or a light pat on the back might assist express this message while also letting them know you care. The key thing is to contact your friend or loved one and let them know you care about them.

Let them know you're here for them
When someone is undergoing a depressive episode, they may believe that no one in the world knows what they are going through.

While you may not understand what depression is like, you may reassure your friends that they do not have to face it alone.

According to research, people tend to retreat when they are depressed. Reaching out to a buddy in need is an important first step. If your loved one isn't ready to chat, you can still express your support by spending time with them. Make sure to check up on them regularly, you can do this over the phone, in person, or via SMS. It will mean a lot to your friends to know that you are always there for them.

Ask how you can help them
Depression seems like a heavy burden that has been placed on your shoulders, both physically and mentally. It can also make a person feel depleted and exhausted. Inquire with your friend about how you may be supportive and helpful during this time. Perhaps you might offer to grab their groceries, sit with them and watch TV, or drive them to an appointment.

It's crucial to be explicit because many people suffering from depression may be hesitant to receive care. Instead of asking "how can I help?" you may ask "Can I come over this weekend to mow your lawn? Listen to their response and proceed from there. Remember that what you offer may not meet their true needs. Support them in a way that will improve their condition.

Encourage them to seek expert help
Depression treatments are vital for depression rehabilitation. However, many people are embarrassed or guilty about their disease and may not feel comfortable obtaining treatment. Others might believe that treatment is ineffective. Regardless of how they feel, encourage your loved one to consult a doctor or therapist to help them manage their depression.

Ask them if they want to discuss
Sometimes the finest thing you can do is simply listen. Be a shoulder to lean on, and create a secure and supportive environment to relieve any stress or pent-up emotions. It's crucial to listen without

interrupting. While you may be tempted to provide advice to "fix problems," doing so may make your friend feel worse or useless. Individuals who are depressed may simply need to talk without receiving unsolicited advice, no matter how noble the intentions. Listening can help them cope with their depression.

Remind them they're not alone
While your friend may feel isolated, depression is widespread. According to the World Health Organization (WHO), depression is a widespread disorder globally, affecting an estimated 3.8% of the population, including 5.0% of adults and 5.7% of those over the age of 60. Globally, about 300 million people suffer from depression.

Remind your friend that the physiological imbalances linked with depression are causing them to feel this way in specific settings. They are neither weak nor faulty. Depression, like heart disease, is considered a sickness. You can also assure them that there is hope. Depression, like all other medical illnesses, can be treated. With the correct combination of drugs and therapy, patients have a good chance of feeling better again.

What not to say
Many people with depression already feel ashamed and guilty about how their symptoms affect those around them. With this in mind, there are some things that you will want to avoid saying when talking to a loved one who is depressed, such as:

- ❖ *Blaming the person for their depression by saying, "It's all in your brain.*
- ❖ *Dismissing their feelings by saying, "it's not that bad" or "you have no right to be depressed."*
- ❖ *Calling them selfish for feeling the way they do by saying, "You only care about yourself"*
- ❖ *Giving them false hope by promising them "it will pass" or "everything will be alright"*

The best thing you can do is be present, open, and nonjudgmental. Do not avoid the individual or their symptoms, even if you are frustrated or helpless. And, while it may be tempting, don't try to take control of their lives.

Instead, attempt to understand your friend or family member's needs, meet them where they are, and discover ways to empower them to receive the care they require.

Chapter 3

Providing Practical Support

Helping someone with depression can be difficult. If someone you know is depressed, you may feel helpless and unsure of what to do. Learn how to support and understand them, as well as how to assist them in obtaining the necessary resources. The more you study about depression, how it affects people, and how to cure it, the more you'll be able to help others. Here is what you can do.

People who suffer from depression may be unaware of or unwilling to admit their condition. They may be unaware of depression's symptoms and believe their feelings are normal.

People frequently feel ashamed of their depression, believing that they can cure it just through effort. However, depression seldom improves without treatment and may sometimes worsen. It is possible to recover with the appropriate treatment. Here's how you can help:

- ❖ *Tell the person what you've seen and why you're worried.*
- ❖ *Explain that depression is a medical problem, not a personal flaw or weakness and that it typically improves with therapy.*
- ❖ *Suggest that you seek expert aid. A healthcare provider is an excellent place to begin. You could also consult a mental health professional, such as a qualified counselor or psychologist.*
- ❖ *Offer to assist in the preparation of a list of questions to be discussed during the initial consultation with a health care professional or mental health practitioner.*
- ❖ *Set up appointments, attend family therapy sessions, and demonstrate your willingness to help.*

If an individual's depression is severe or potentially life-threatening, they should see a doctor, a mental health professional, or an emergency medical service.

Watch for indicators of deepening depression.

People may feel depression in a variety of ways. Observe someone suffering from depression to learn how it affects them. Consider the following issues:

- ❖ *What are typical indications of depression?*
- ❖ *What habits or language do you notice as depression worsens?*
- ❖ *What behaviors or language do you observe when this individual is performing well?*
- ❖ *What causes episodes of more acute depression?*
- ❖ *What activities are most effective when depression worsens?*

Severe depression should be treated as soon as feasible. Encourage a person with depression to collaborate with a health care or mental health practitioner to develop a plan for what to do when symptoms worsen, including who to call. In some circumstances, the provider may need to tweak or replace medications or suggest other treatments.

Understand the risk of suicide

Depression puts people at a higher risk of suicide. If someone is really depressed, they may consider suicide at some point. Take any indicators of ending it seriously and act swiftly. Take action as needed:

Call a suicide hotline

Request advice and information about available resources in your region. Alternatively, encourage the person at risk to call a hotline for help.

In the United States, dial or text 988 to contact the 988 Suicide & Crisis Lifeline. It is open 24 hours a day, every day, or you can use the Lifeline Chat.

Veterans and service members in trouble in the United States can contact the Veterans Trouble Line by dialing 988 and pressing "1". Or texting 838255. Alternatively, you can talk online.

Ensure the person's safety
If at all feasible, take out everything that could be a way to put a stop to it all. For example, remove or secure firearms, other weapons, and medications.

Dial your local emergency number immediately if you think someone is about to hurt them. Make sure that someone is always with the person.

Stay vigilant for warning indications of suicide
Learn and be aware of the following typical warning signs of such ideation:

- ❖ *Having a conversation about suicide means expressing words like "I wish I were dead," "I'm going to kill myself," or "I wish I hadn't been born."*
- ❖ *Withdrawing from social interaction and preferring to be left alone.*
- ❖ *Experiencing mood swings, such as being emotionally elated one day and depressed and irritated the next.*
- ❖ *Getting lost in thoughts of death, dying, or violence.*
- ❖ *Feeling stuck or despondent in a circumstance.*
- ❖ *Increasing consumption of alcohol or drugs.*
- ❖ *Changing the typical schedule, such as eating or sleeping habits.*
- ❖ *Engaging in risky or self-destructive behavior, such as drug use or irresponsible driving.*
- ❖ *Donating possessions or tidying up when it serves no purpose.*
- ❖ *Saying goodbye to someone as if they might never be seen again.*

Experiencing personality changes or feeling extremely nervous or agitated, particularly in conjunction with some of the warning indications listed above.

Show support
Remember that depression is nobody's fault. You cannot cure someone's depression, but your support and understanding can help.
You can do:

Encourage the person to continue with treatment.
If someone is in depression treatment, help them remember to take
their medications and keep their appointments.

Be willing to listen
Tell them that you want to know how they feel. Pay close attention
while they speak. However, do not offer advice or ideas, and do not
judge them. Simply listening and understanding can be effective
therapeutic techniques.

Provide positive encouragement
People who are depressed may harshly assess themselves and
criticize everything they do. Remind them of their great
characteristics and how important they are to you and others.

Offer assistance
A person may be unable to perform some duties well. Suggest
particular tasks that you would be willing to complete. Ask whether
you can take on a specific assignment.

Help to make their lives less stressful
Developing a regular schedule can help a person with depression
feel more in control. Offer to create a food, medicine, physical
activity, social support, and sleep regimen, as well as assist with
domestic duties organization.

Find useful organizations
Many organizations provide support groups, counseling, and other
depression-related services. For example, the National Alliance on
Mental Illness, employee assistance programs, and many faith-
based organizations provide aid with mental health issues.

Encourage them to actively participate in their faith, if it is a part of
their lives. Faith is a significant aspect of many people's depression
treatment, whether it's through participation in an organized religious
organization or personal spiritual beliefs and practices.

Encourage the individual to take self-care steps

This involves eating healthy meals, getting enough sleep, and exercising regularly.

Make plans together
Invite the person to go on a walk with you, see a movie, or work with you on a past interest or hobby. But don't try to push them to do anything.

Chapter 4

Encourage Treatment And Recovery

There are ways to urge them to seek assistance; however, you do not want to appear as if you are attempting to push or pressure them, as this may drive them to refuse. Instead, you should gently advise that they seek assistance while allowing them to make the final decision.

When considering treatment for depression with someone suffering from it, consider the following:

Know what therapy alternatives are available.
Before discussing treatment with them, look into local mental health doctors, treatment clinics, and support groups. You can even contact ahead to inquire about the admissions procedure, but you should not schedule an appointment without authorization.

Ask the person if they are willing to receive assistance
Rather than asking that they seek assistance, inquire whether it is something they would consider. If they are hesitant, remind them that they can take some time to think about it. Don't put pressure on them to make a decision right away.

If they appear resistive, ask why without passing judgment.
They may say they are afraid, unclear of how to seek help, or hopeless that treatment will help them. Depending on their response, you can offer support, comfort, and additional information to alleviate their anxieties.

Find out whether there is anything you can do to assist.
If they are unsure, you can make ideas, such as assisting them in scheduling an appointment or accompanying them to their first consultation.

What treatments include

Depression may be treated with individual, group, or family therapy, as well as medicine. Treatments for severe depression that work well include cognitive behavioral therapy (CBT) and interpersonal therapy. Interpersonal therapy improves a person's communication and connections. CBT assists a person in developing new coping strategies and changing negative ideas and beliefs.

There are lots of medications available to help treat depression ranging from different antidepressants, and these are a type of drug that can help reduce it. Antidepressants are classified into numerous kinds, which include:

Tricyclic antidepressants include Anafranil (clomipramine), Tofranil (imipramine), and Elavil (amitriptyline).

Sertraline (Zoloft), paroxetine (Paxil), and fluoxetine (Prozac) are examples of SSRIs.

Serotonin and norepinephrine reuptake inhibitors (SNRIs) include duloxetine (Cymbalta) and desvenlafaxine (Pristiq).

To learn more about depression drugs, schedule an appointment with a psychiatrist, psychiatric nurse practitioner, or another healthcare provider who is licensed to prescribe antidepressants.

Support groups are another therapeutic approach. Depending on the group, it could be led by a mental health professional or a peer in recovery. The National Alliance on Mental Illness (NAMI) offers in-person and online support groups to anyone struggling with a mental health issue.

Even if your friend or family member seeks treatment for depression, you can continue to support them. If you're not sure how to help, ask them how they want you to support them during this time. Depending on their comfort level, they may invite you to participate in their treatment by attending therapy sessions or appointments. Others may choose to seek assistance on their own, but ask that you call or check in with them.

If you believe you are contributing to the person's depression, you may want to seek professional help. For example, if you suffer from addiction, high stress, or mental health concerns, you may be unaware of how your personal struggles are affecting your loved one. If this is the case, you could benefit from counseling, therapy, or support groups.

In other circumstances, a loved one may deny their sadness or refuse to get help. Witnessing someone you love suffer can be tough. If the individual does not wish to seek assistance, consider the following:

Respect their decision.
While you may disagree, continuing to force your advice on someone may simply make them more resistant to seeking treatment. Instead, try to accept that this is their decision without giving up totally. Remind them that if they change their mind, you are available to assist.

Maintain appropriate boundaries to avoid enabling behavior
Enabling occurs when you reinforce someone's conduct, frequently without realizing it. For example, you could cover for someone you care about if they miss work. Enabling removes the negative consequences of the individual's conduct. When a loved one's depression interferes with several aspects of their life, avoid jumping in to save them.

Suggest family treatment
If your family members are unwilling to seek help on their own, they may be willing to see a professional alongside you. Family relationships can contribute to depression, so seeking assistance as a family might be beneficial. Your family members may also feel less pressured if they are not the only ones receiving assistance.

Seek therapy or a support group for yourself
Having someone you care about deal with depression can be
unpleasant, so you may want to seek help as well. NAMI offers
information and assistance to family members and caregivers of
people with mental illnesses. They also provide family support
groups in person and online.

Chapter 5

Self-Care For Caregivers

Taking care of a loved one, whether it's a child, partner, family, or friend, can leave you as exhausted, in pain, and frustrated as they are. Having a difficult time while a loved one is coping with mental health concerns can be like a guilty secret: it exists, but no one wants to admit it. Unfortunately, there are often little services available to caretakers. That may cause you to try to disguise your discomfort, which just makes matters worse.

For someone suffering from depression, life can be a daily struggle. What appears to be giving in on the outside frequently feels like a continual struggle on the inside; for example, when you're depressed, getting out of bed, dressing, and going to the grocery store can require a lot of effort. It can be difficult for someone who wants to aid the sufferer to find out how to do so. Your fantastic ideas for motivating and distracting your loved one may feel too difficult for them, and they may perceive you as pushing too hard or setting unrealistic expectations.

Many times, their mood will affect your day, and you may experience some of the same symptoms. If they wake up feeling upbeat, you can breathe a sigh of relief because your mood may be similar. If they come home from work in a bad mood, you may feel like your night is wrecked. Consumed with watching their emotional temperature, they can feel like a tidal wave that takes you away.

The most difficult thing is that you are not supposed to be in agony because you did not receive the diagnosis. When you suffer your own symptoms, you may characterize yourself as petty or selfish in addition to receiving little support or attention. When that happens, it's like adding insult to injury; in addition to dealing with the challenges of your circumstance, you're angry at yourself for not being a Superman or a saint and rising above every difficulty and reaction. You are not alone. Many caregivers develop burnout.

Here are some of the symptoms:

Fear for the Future
One of the primary concerns while living with someone who is
suffering is, "Will this ever end? The person you know in the past
appears to be gone. Your shared future goals are in peril. Your role
has changed. This is not what you signed up for, and you are not
sure you can manage it indefinitely.

The good news about depression is that there is always hope for
change. If the condition is brought on by a sudden sickness, injury,
or trauma, their mood may improve as the situation stabilizes. If your
loved one has long struggled with depression and it has lately
worsened, the correct combination of drugs, therapy, and coping
skills is likely to reduce the severity.

You may never entirely rid your life of depression. However, it is a
cyclical state, with ups and downs, so it rarely remains constant. So,
while there is no answer to the question "How long will this last?",
you can count on experiencing better times and, in many cases,
stabilizing.

Desire for Escape
No one wants to leave the person they love, but when that person
continually acts negative or helpless, it's a normal reaction. And a
natural one. Remember that feelings are not the same as facts, you
can be rebellious and think about leaving, but be responsible and
stay put.

If you feel confined, unable to leave, or even take some time off, you
should seek as much support as possible. If you have the resources,
hiring caregivers or alternative healers can help not only jumpstart
your loved one's recovery but also provide you with some much-
needed rest. You will require the assistance of a team, whether it is
made up of paid professionals or friends and family. Hire a massage
therapist, personal trainer, or life coach. Invite a friend to play cards,
read books aloud, or cook dinner. Your desire to distance yourself is

normal and a clear indication that you are suffering from compassion fatigue, as described by therapists.

Want to "Fix" Your Loved One
If seeking solutions makes you feel more productive, it can be beneficial to investigate all possible pathways of recovery, such as EMDR (eye movement desensitization and reprocessing), TMS (transcranial magnetic stimulation), vitamins, and electroshock. Many have helped those who had tried other options without success.

If you've exhausted all of your options or don't have the resources to keep trying new things, you can quickly become discouraged. Acceptance is key here, as is avoiding black-and-white, all-or-nothing thinking. Your loved one will not always behave like this. You may need to take a break from "fixing" before moving on to fresh ideas. Or you might need to embrace a more tolerant point of view, a sense that if this is "the new normal," maybe there are ways to make it bearable.

Anger and Guilt
The top two feelings experienced by caretakers are anger and guilt, which are two sides of the same coin. Anger is the most active of the reactions, and it might be directed toward a loved one, the ailment, yourself, God, or doctors. Everyone who is exhausted, nervous, or worn out will eventually become angry.

From the outside, resenting your loved one makes sense. It is a terrible feature of depression because it causes people to feel helpless and hopeless, making them appear unmotivated from the outside. As a caretaker, knowing that your wife isn't doing the things that have been given to her, such as exercise, medicine, or socializing, can appear to be a lack of effort, leaving you dissatisfied and powerless.

Try to interpret your shame as a misguided indication of how much you care. Then practice more self-care to help you get through these challenging emotions. It's typical, albeit misguided, to blame yourself for your loved one's situation. You may persuade yourself that you didn't do enough to prevent it or that you aren't making enough sacrifices to accommodate them. Each social event or night out becomes a minefield of regret.

Most importantly, you may feel terrible for all of the aforementioned feelings, particularly rage, because you care deeply about the person and want to assist. Try to interpret your shame as a misguided indication of how much you care. Then practice more self-care to help you get through these challenging emotions.

I hope you can see from this list that the aggregate of all of these sensations leads to tiredness and burnout. However, if you find yourself in this situation, there are steps you may take to regain control over your life.

How to Look Out for Yourself.

You need self-care just as much as your partner.
When they struggle, you too struggle. Your discomfort is equally important. Self-care benefits them in two ways. First, you're developing your strength, patience, and capacity to care for them. Second, you are modeling the abilities that your loved one needs to improve. Setting a good example might help to motivate and inspire others.

Set Boundaries
It's fine to say no. Even if your loved one is unable to handle their own life, you are not solely responsible for it. Decide for yourself how you can best support them, and leave the rest undone. Perhaps you are skilled in finance or cooking and wish to take over those responsibilities. Perhaps you can identify the most important needs and are willing to address them. But remember that you cannot and should not do everything. You can help the depressed individual by insisting that they take some responsibility for their own life. They can remain motivated and focused as a result. So, when it's reasonable, not during a big breakdown, demand some reciprocity.

Be mindful, and practice acceptance
Many people try to cope with discomfort by either worrying about it (fight) or distancing themselves from it (flight). Surprisingly, modern approaches suggest that sitting with negative emotions is the quickest way to overcome them. although anxiety is worried about the future and depression is unhappy about the past, the present moment is usually better, although not perfect. You may deal with difficult circumstances with more patience and less anguish by adopting some mindfulness principles, such as being in the moment and not judging your reactions.

Try not to buy into the distorted thoughts
When we're thinking negatively (stinkin' thinkin'), our ideas tend to fall into the same negative slots repeatedly. Experts refer to this as cognitive distortions, which include leaping to the worst conceivable conclusions, perceiving the world in all-or-nothing terms, and blaming. Being able to name those thoughts as erroneous or indicators of depression allows us to place less value on exaggerations and think more objectively.

Get help and support for yourself
If you're becoming increasingly angry, getting ill more frequently, or not seeing your friends for weeks, these are all signals that you need more. More activity, rest, and, most importantly, more people around you. If you don't want to take the professional way, you might be amazed at how much assistance your friends and family members are prepared to provide. If you want to speak with someone impartial, therapists can provide a safe space for you to express your emotions.

Finally, caregiver support groups provide a safe area where everyone understands and empathizes with your situation. Whatever you decide, keep in mind that support is accessible and that reaching out is not only acceptable but frequently required.

Conclusion

Depression, like heart disease and diabetes, is a prevalent but treatable medical problem. Knowing the indications of depression is the first step toward getting them the care they need.

It's easy to feel overwhelmed, disappointed, and helpless when someone you care about is depressed or you suspect they are but don't know for sure. For starters, it's critical to understand the distinction between feeling depressed and having a more serious mental health problem that requires therapy.

Feeling down is frequently a short setback brought on by an external incident, such as a disagreement with a family member or a failure at work. It does not impede day-to-day functioning for an extended amount of time, and someone experiencing this will usually continue to engage in things they enjoy after a few days or a week at most.

Surprising Facts about Major Depression Disorder

Major depression is common all over the world, yet there are still misconceptions about the diagnosis. In contrast, clinical depression is characterized by symptoms such as withdrawing from friends and losing interest in previously enjoyed activities, which last for a significantly longer period of time. To be diagnosed with clinical depression, symptoms must last at least two weeks and indicate a change in one's previous level of functioning.

People suffering from depression have a totally different attitude than others who are feeling low. When a person is down, they frequently hope that things will improve. "The individual suffering from depression believes that their condition is hopeless and cannot be improved.

Signs and symptoms to watch for in a loved one include the following:

- ❖ *Expressing emotions of melancholy, emptiness, or pessimism*
- ❖ *Feeling impatient, frustrated, or upset over minor issues.*
- ❖ *Sleeping significantly more or less than average*
- ❖ *Feeling anxious, restless, or agitated.*
- ❖ *Have inexplicable bodily concerns, such as back discomfort or headaches.*
- ❖ *Difficulty thinking, concentrating, remembering, and making judgments.*
- ❖ *Expressing sentiments of remorse or worthlessness, or reflecting on previous failures*
- ❖ *Mentioning death or suicidal ideation.*

If someone you care about has been confirmed to have depression or exhibits any of these signs, knowing how to respond is critical. Here are six ways to help.

Bring Your Concerns to Your Loved One
If you observe indicators of depression in a loved one, convey your concerns quietly and nonjudgmentally. It's also important to give your loved one space to express their emotions.

Listening is the most critical aspect in starting to help. To get them talking, start by noting any recent changes that have worried you. When you do this, don't be critical; instead, express the facts as you perceive them in a neutral tone, pausing frequently to allow them to reply to what you're saying.

Avoid suggesting that they have no reason to be so miserable. This includes avoiding saying things like, "Look at all the positive things in your life" or "Look at how much more serious so-and-so is, but she doesn't let her troubles get her down.

Many people suffering from depression believe they should be able to snap out of it or be psychologically strong, which can prevent them from seeking therapy for depression.

Help Your Loved One Get Treatment
Someone suffering from depression may require assistance in seeking care, both due to a sense of stigma or shame, and because their disease makes it difficult for them to manage duties such as finding a mental health practitioner

or organizing an appointment. Suggesting that you can do these things for them, reminding them of their upcoming appointment, and accompanying them to the visit can help them receive treatment sooner rather than later.

Whether they're afraid to see a mental health expert, such as a psychologist or psychiatrist, ask whether they'd be willing to see their primary care doctor, especially if they already know and trust them. Although it is preferable to consult someone who specializes in mental health, the most crucial aspect is getting connected to some type of assistance when necessary.

You may also need to reconsider the terms you use while discussing depression treatment, as various people may perceive the problem differently. For example, some people might not know how to describe how they feel when they're sad and instead think of their symptoms as "stressed out" or "not myself," for example.

When attempting to intervene, it is critical to match the language that the person understands.

Support their daily routine
While initiating therapy is an important step toward treating depression, your loved one may still require assistance with daily tasks. Offering to accompany them to a therapy appointment so that they may hear directly from their mental healthcare provider is one method to help.

In order to get them out and about, you might also offer to help them with tasks that could seem burdensome, like housecleaning, laundry, or grocery shopping. You could even suggest that you go for a little stroll around the neighborhood.

Establishing a habit is also really beneficial. You may try to go for a walk every day, for example. Regular physical activity helps reduce stress and release endorphins and other neurotransmitters, or chemicals in the brain, which aid in improving mood.

Behavioral activation is one type of depression treatment that involves engaging in activities that are meaningful to you, such as completing a pleasurable form of exercise or volunteering.

Encourage your loved one to participate in activities that provide them personal happiness, but don't overdo it with activities and socializing. Most people try to repair the situation by forcing their loved ones to participate in activities and interact. This is not always a good thing because it might increase stress and unintentionally worsen symptoms.

Seek indications that the medication is having an effect
There are numerous subtle signs that treatment is working; these will be evident in how your loved one seems and behaves. As they improve, someone suffering from depression may begin to make better eye contact with you rather than glancing down to avoid eye contact owing to feelings of vulnerability or anxiety. Other indicators of improvement include:

- ❖ *Smiling sometimes and having more relaxed rather than strained facial characteristics.*
- ❖ *Have a calmer demeanor.*
- ❖ *Reducing isolation and increasing interaction with others*
- ❖ *Eating and sleeping well.*

Be Alert to Signs That Treatment Isn't Working
On the other hand, the absence of any such signals indicates that one's depression is not improving and may be worsening, with the primary concern in the absence of improvement being whether your loved one is experiencing thoughts of taking their life.

At this point, you should gently bring up the question of whether they ever considered whether their life wasn't worth living. The following are indications that your loved one may be thinking of ending it:

- ❖ *Buying a firearm or hoarding pills*
- ❖ *Focusing on violence, death, or dying.*
- ❖ *withdrawing from social contact with others.*
- ❖ *Feeling despondent or imprisoned in their present circumstances.*
- ❖ *Telling them, "goodbye," as if they'll disappear*
- ❖ *Arranging their business or selling their possessions without providing a valid justification*

If your loved one exhibits signs of preparing to end it, take the following steps to lessen the chance:

Make every effort to persuade them to visit a specialist if they haven't already, and make sure to accompany them to the appointment.
Consider an alternative approach to therapy.
Remove any guns from the house.

Ensure that they are not stockpiling medications that could be used in an overdose. If you notice indicators of this behavior in your loved one, treat it as an emergency and rush them to the hospital or contact an ambulance.

If you are concerned that your loved one's condition is deteriorating but they are not planning or exhibiting any harmful conduct, ask to accompany them for a portion of their next psychiatric or counseling session or express your concerns to their provider. You may advise that you attend frequent counseling sessions with their physician or therapist. This will allow you to provide input on how treatment appears to be working, listen to what your loved one and their doctor are saying, and better understand how you might be able to help.

Create a Plan for Recognizing a Relapse.
When you're in a long-term relationship with someone who has depression, it's vital to remember that depression is frequently a chronic illness with symptoms that flare up on occasion, just like medical disorders like heart disease or diabetes.

Knowing and accepting that there will be ups and downs will assist reduce any personal frustration that may arise when dealing with a depressed loved one. Individual therapy may be beneficial for family members or loved ones who are caring for a depressed person in order to help them cope with the person's mood.

Although depressive episodes can be treated well, the possibility of future relapses can have a negative impact on relationships. That is why it is critical to speak with your loved one while they are in remission so that you can devise a strategy for recognizing and responding swiftly when a relapse is imminent.

Recognizing the early warning symptoms is critical for a gentle intervention. You can also promote lifestyle choices that may help prevent depression, such as:

- ❖ *Healthy eating and exercise habits.*
- ❖ *Minimizing stress*
- ❖ *Getting lots of sleep*
- ❖ *Limiting alcohol and drug use.*
- ❖ *Sticking to any depression strategies for treatment for therapy or medication.*